LET'S MAKE HISTORY

The Ancient World

Paul Titley

Illustrations by Ken Petts
Models and diagrams by Hilary Evans

OWLET BOOKS
London·Sydney·Toronto

AN EARLY HARPOON

About 11 000 years ago people lived near the village of Les Eyzies in southwest France. They had learned how to make bone needles, scrape skins with flint scrapers, and sew tents and clothes. They had also learned how to make barbed harpoons out of reindeer bone.

The barbs were made by cutting into the bone with a sharpened flint. The barb was then fastened to a wooden javelin with animal sinew. These harpoons could probably have been used for hunting, but would have been more effective for fishing in the nearby River Vezere.

It is interesting that these harpoons were made of reindeer bone. This was the time of the last Ice Age in Europe. As the ice retreated and the weather got warmer, the reindeer moved further north.

How to make the harpoon

Materials: pencil, garden cane, string, craft knife, paint, brush

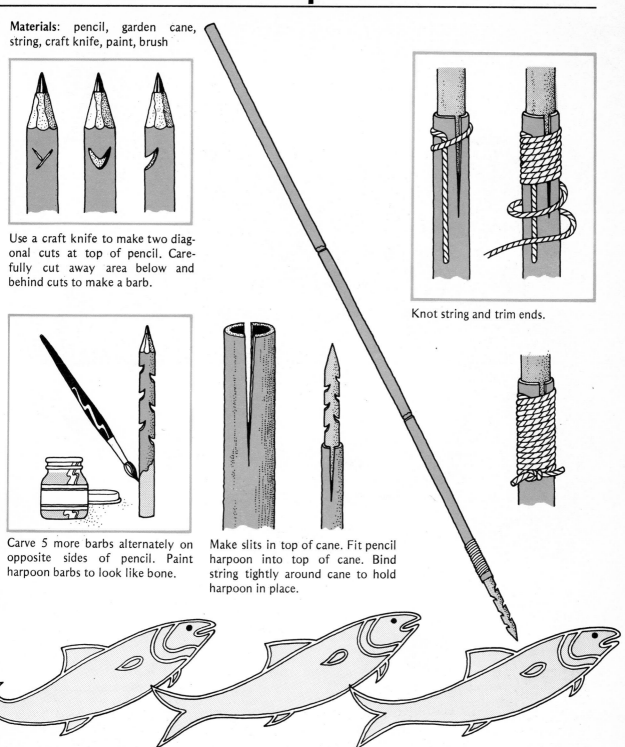

Use a craft knife to make two diagonal cuts at top of pencil. Carefully cut away area below and behind cuts to make a barb.

Carve 5 more barbs alternately on opposite sides of pencil. Paint harpoon barbs to look like bone.

Make slits in top of cane. Fit pencil harpoon into top of cane. Bind string tightly around cane to hold harpoon in place.

Knot string and trim ends.

3

A STONE AGE AXE

About 5000 B.C. farmers in Europe were using axes made of flint. Flint is brittle and can be chipped into its final shape by using another piece of flint. The edges can be sharpened by grinding them on a flat sandstone. Skilled flintworkers could produce very sharp tools.

The earliest axes were just pieces of sharpened flint held in the hand. Gradually, people learned how to drill a wooden handle with a pointed stone and then force the flint axehead in until it held securely.

Although flint axes needed to be replaced quite frequently, they could be used for clearing small trees and preparing timber for house building.

How to make the axe

Materials: modelling clay, covered corrugated cardboard, craft knife, string, paint, paintbrush

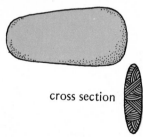

cross section

Model axe blade from clay. Don't make it too thick in the middle.

When axe blade is thoroughly dry, carefully carve cutting edge with craft knife.

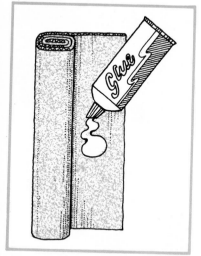

Cut rectangle of covered corrugated cardboard. Fold over 1 edge and roll up to form axe handle. Glue edges. Paint handle to look like wood.

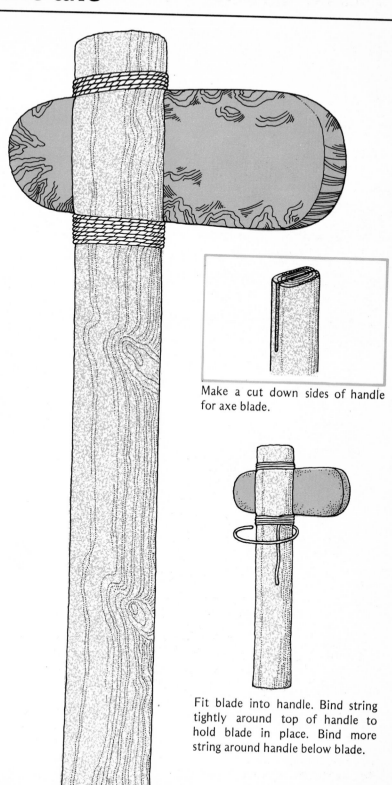

Make a cut down sides of handle for axe blade.

Fit blade into handle. Bind string tightly around top of handle to hold blade in place. Bind more string around handle below blade.

A CORACLE

A coracle was one of the earliest boats. It was designed in the shape of a shallow, wide-mouthed basket, measuring about one and a half metres by one metre.

The boat builder first made a skeleton frame by interweaving six laths at right angles with another six laths. The ends of the frame were bent upwards and fastened to the gunwale. The gunwhale was usually made of plaited willow branches. The boat was then covered with hides and coated with pitch to make it waterproof. The seat was a plank wedged into the coracle.

Coracles similar to these are still used by a few fishermen on the rivers of southwest Wales.

How to make the coracle

Materials: cardboard, tissue paper, wallpaper paste, glue, scissors, ruler, pencil, enamel paint, paintbrush

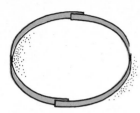

Cut 8 cardboard strips 35 x 1cm. Glue 2 strips together to form oval.

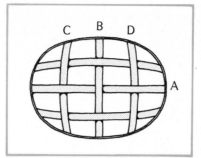

Glue on 1 strip on each side of A, threading them under C and D and over B.

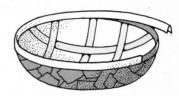

Cut long cardboard strip 2cm wide. Score down centre and fold in half. Glue strip around top of coracle.

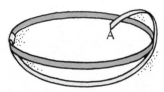

Glue strip A onto oval. Do not make coracle deeper than 6cm at centre.

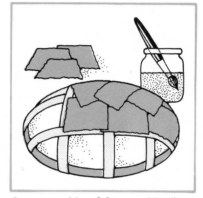

Cover outside of frame with pieces of tissue paper. Glue on with wallpaper paste. Glue on four more layers of tissue paper.

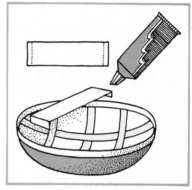

For seat, cut cardboard rectangle 4cm wide and as long as coracle width plus 1cm. Fold ends over to fit into coracle. Glue in place. Paint coracle with black enamel paint. It will float only if enamel paint is used.

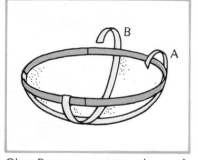

Glue B across centre oval over A.

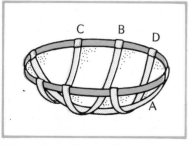

Glue strips C and D across oval threading them under A.

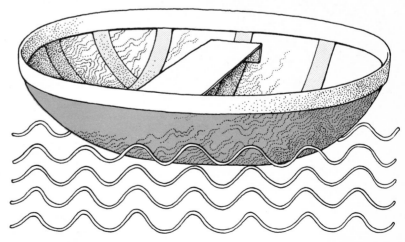

STONEHENGE

It is thought that Stonehenge on Salisbury Plain was a Bronze Age centre for sun worship. It consists of two large stone circles surrounding two horseshoe shaped groupings, in the middle of which is a large stone called the altar stone.

Geologically, the stones are of two types. The very large stones are Sarsen stones, and the smaller ones are bluestones.

The Sarsen stones came from a quarry 32 kilometres north of Stonehenge. After they were quarried, they were dressed to the right size and shape. As this could only have been done by pounding them with other stones, it must

have taken many years. The dressed stones were dragged to the site on tree trunks.

To erect each pillar a hole 1 to 2 metres deep was dug and the stone slowly raised. When it was almost upright teams of men hauled on the ropes until it fell into place. Then the pillar tops were made an even height, and tenons gouged out to hold the lintels. The lintels were probably raised on timber ramps.

The bluestones were quarried in the Prescelly Mountains in Wales. They were brought as far as possible by water, probably on rafts. Overland they would have been transported in the same way as the Sarsen stones.

How to make Stonehenge

Materials: cardboard, cellulose filler, modelling clay, plastic comb, glue, compasses, knife, ruler, pencil, paint, paintbrush

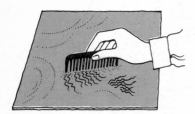

Make base for model from 36cm square of cardboard. Mix cellulose filler with water and spread it thinly over base. Do not make surface too uneven or the stones will not stand upright. When base is dry, paint it grass green.

Make all stones from modelling clay. First model 30 outer ring Sarsen stones 5 x 2 x 1cm. Shape stones to taper slightly at top. Make 30 lintels for outer ring 5mm high, 2.8cm wide and 1cm deep.

Make 10 large Sarsen stones 7cm high, 2.5cm wide and just over 1cm deep. Taper these at top to 1.5cm. Model 5 lintels 5mm high, 4cm wide, and 1cm deep, one for each pair of stones.

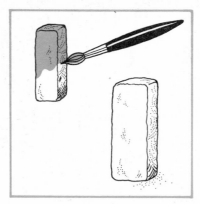

The inner ring and horseshoe grouping are small blue stones 2cm x 5mm x 5mm. Make 45 for inner ring and 17 for horseshoe grouping. When dry, paint stones blue-grey.

Finally, make altar stone 3cm high, 1cm wide, and 5mm deep.

Allow all clay stones to dry thoroughly before gluing them onto base.

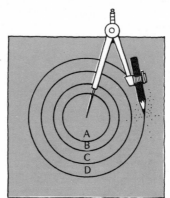

Using compasses, draw 4 circles 27cm, 21cm, 15cm and 11cm in diameter on base.

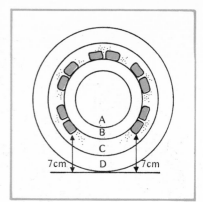

Glue 5 pairs of large Sarsen stones in horseshoe shape on circle B. If textured surface is too uneven, scrape it smooth before gluing on stones. Glue a lintel over each pair of stones

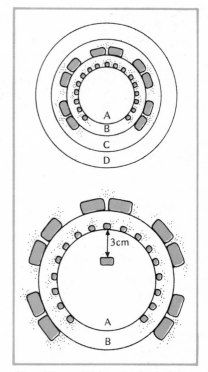

Glue 17 small blue stones in horseshoe shape following line of circle A. Glue altar stone 3cm from middle blue stone.

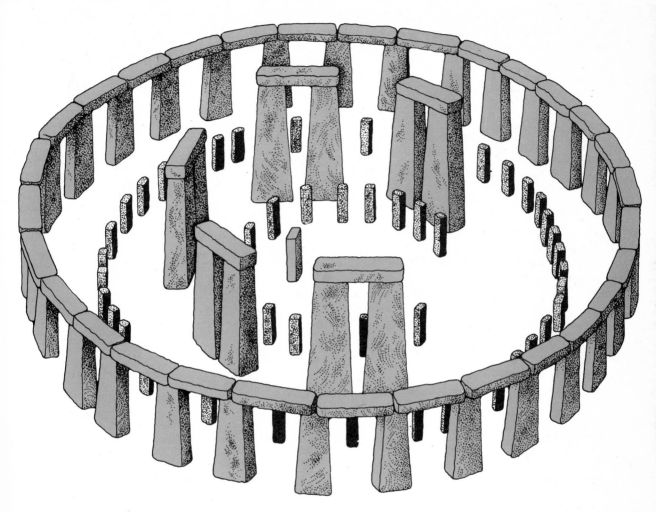

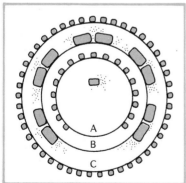

Space remaining 45 blue stones evenly around circle C. Glue them onto the base.

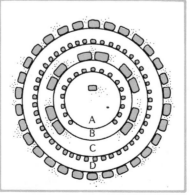

Space 30 Sarsen stones evenly around circle D and glue to base.

Glue lintels across tops of stones. Paint over any pencil marks.

AN EARLY WHEELED CART

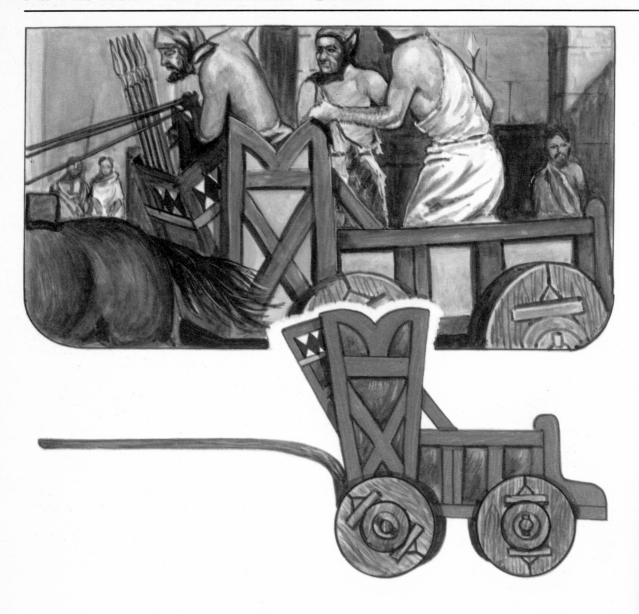

No one knows exactly when, where or by whom the wheel was invented. However, it is generally agreed by historians that the first wheeled carts were in use in the Middle East about 4000 B.C.

The first wheels were made of three separate pieces of wood joined together by two wooden bars. The whole uneven circle was probably bound with a form of leather tyre. The centre piece of wood had a hole bored in it through which the axle went. The axle was fixed by wooden pins. The axle turned with the wheel and the base of the cart had to be fastened on with loose leather thongs.

How to make the cart

Materials: small cardboard box, cardboard, thin wooden dowel, glue, pencil, ruler, craft knife, compasses, paint, paintbrush

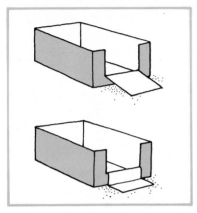

Find a small cardboard box—the inside of a large matchbox is ideal. Make 2 cuts in one end of box and fold to form a step. Glue step to box.

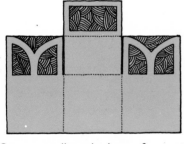

Cut a cardboard shape for cart front. It should fit across cart front and halfway down sides. Cut out shaded areas and score along dotted lines.

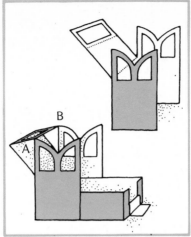

Fold front into shape. Glue together at A and B. Glue front to box.

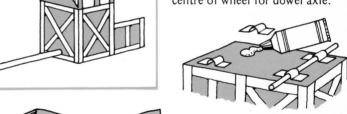

Cut some cardboard strips and glue them on cart front and sides. Cut a piece of dowel 1½ times cart's length for shaft. Make a small hole in cart front. Push dowel through hole and glue to cart.

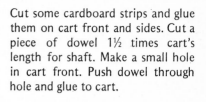

Cut 8 cardboard circles for wheels. Use 2 circles for each wheel. Cut 1 circle into 3 pieces and glue them onto complete circle. Glue 2 cardboard strips across the pieces. Cut a thin cardboard strip and glue it around wheel rim. Make a hole in centre of wheel for dowel axle.

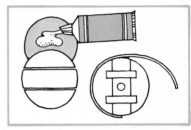

Cut 4 cardboard strips for loops to hold axle. Bend them into shape and glue them onto cart base. Cut 2 pieces of dowel for axles. Push them through cardboard loops. Glue wheels to axles. Paint cart.

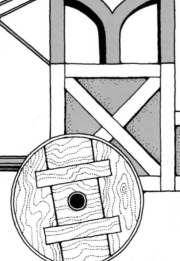

AN EGYPTIAN WAR CHARIOT

Egyptian war chariots were made of light pieces of wood set into a framework of metal strips. The axle was at the rear of the chariot, which enabled the driver to make sudden turns at speed without great risk of overturning. Spoked wheels had been invented and these were lighter and faster than solid wheels.

War chariots were drawn by two horses and carried two men, a driver and an archer. The chariots were particularly effective in charging at rows of foot soldiers, who had little protection against them.

How to make the chariot

Materials: 2 circular box lids 11cm in diameter, cardboard, Plasticine, pencil, ruler, scissors, craft knife, compasses, glue, paint, paintbrush

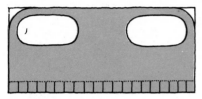

Cut shape for chariot front and sides from cardboard rectangle 12 x 27cm. Score a line across bottom 2cm from edge. Cut slits along bottom up to scored line.

Cut a cardboard base 10 x 12cm. Round 2 corners by cutting away shaded parts. Bend front and sides shape around chariot base. Glue flaps onto base.

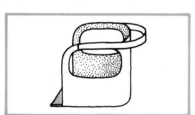

Cut a cardboard strip 25 x 1cm for rail at chariot front. Glue it onto chariot.

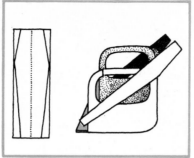

Cut 2 bow holders from cardboard rectangles 18 x 6cm. Score down centre and fold. Glue edges together, but leave top open.

Cut 2 shafts from cardboard rectangles 24 x 3.5cm. Glue pieces together and glue to chariot base.

Cut 2 cardboard strips for loops to hold axle. Glue them to chariot base. Push pencil through loops.

Cut 2 cardboard circles 5cm in diameter. Glue them at centre on insides of circular box lids. Make central holes in wheels for axle. Draw circles 2.5cm in diameter in centre of wheels. Cut out 6 spokes in each wheel. Fit wheels onto axle and glue in place. Make 2 Plasticine hubs and press them over axle ends. Paint and decorate the chariot.

A PHARAOH'S THRONE

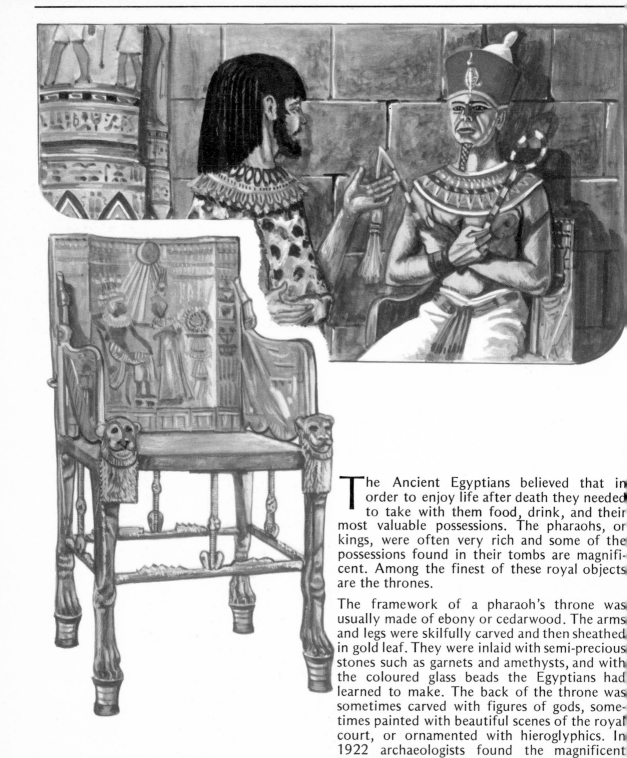

The Ancient Egyptians believed that in order to enjoy life after death they needed to take with them food, drink, and their most valuable possessions. The pharaohs, or kings, were often very rich and some of the possessions found in their tombs are magnificent. Among the finest of these royal objects are the thrones.

The framework of a pharaoh's throne was usually made of ebony or cedarwood. The arms and legs were skilfully carved and then sheathed in gold leaf. They were inlaid with semi-precious stones such as garnets and amethysts, and with the coloured glass beads the Egyptians had learned to make. The back of the throne was sometimes carved with figures of gods, sometimes painted with beautiful scenes of the royal court, or ornamented with hieroglyphics. In 1922 archaeologists found the magnificent royal throne of the boy pharaoh Tutankhamun.

How to make the throne

Materials: tall cardboard box, pieces of plastic foam, cardboard, pencil, ruler, glue, scissors, craft knife, paint, paintbrush

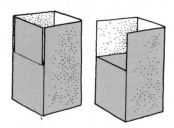

Score a line across box front. Cut sides down to scored line. Fold front into box. Glue onto back to form seat.

Cut sides to form throne arms. Cut some thin cardboard strips. Glue them onto arms and back to cover edges.

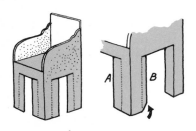

Cut out throne legs, making them twice the finished width. To make each leg, score a line down centre of leg shape. Cut across top to scored line. Fold sections A and B inwards and glue them together to make square leg.

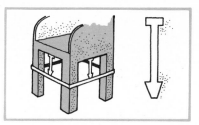

Cut a cardboard strip and glue it around throne legs. Cut 4 cardboard shapes and glue 1 on each side between strip and throne seat.

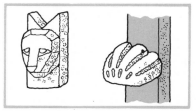

Carve 2 lions' heads and 4 clawed feet from pieces of plastic foam. Glue them to throne.

Paint throne gold. Decorate back and arms.

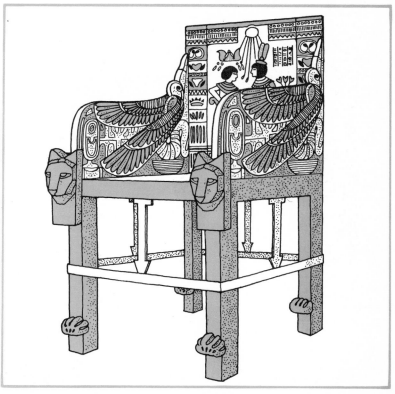

AN EGYPTIAN JEWELLED COLLAR

Egyptian jewellers were very highly skilled craftsmen who had learned how to beat out gold and use a wide variety of semi-precious stones, such as turquoise, red garnets, amethysts, and yellow jasper. They could also make brightly coloured glass-like beads from polished quartz.

Among the finest examples of Egyptian jewellery were the beautiful collars worn by wealthy men and women. The most magnificent of these collars were made of gold leaf inlaid with beads and precious stones. Almost as beautiful were those made of hundreds of jewels strung together with gold wire. The clasps of these collars were often in the shapes of birds' or animals' heads.

How to make the collar

Materials: macaroni, pasta rings, 2 needles, cardboard, ruler, thread, cord, pencil, glue, scissors, paint

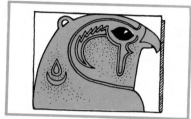

Cut 2 cardboard rectangles 11 x 7cm. Fold in half. Draw on bird's head clasps. Cut out. Paint gold.

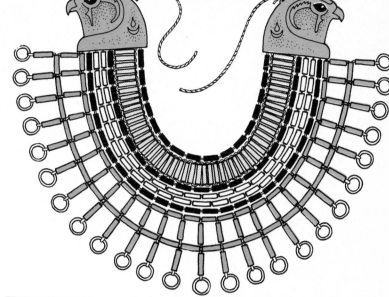

Sort macaroni into pieces of equal length. Discard curved pieces. Thread 1st string of 16 macaroni beads. Leave length of thread at each end. Thread 5 more strings of 21, 22, 23, and two of 24 beads for 3rd, 4th, 5th, 6th, and bottom rows. Leave threads at ends. Tie these in bows.

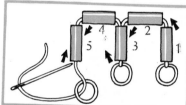

Bottom row: knot a long thread onto a pasta ring. Take thread through 3 beads, through another pasta ring, then **back** through 3rd bead. Thread on 2 more beads (4 and 5) and a ring. Take thread back through 5th bead. Continue threading 2 beads and a ring until 25 rings have been used. Tie thread onto last ring.

Place a 24-bead row above bottom row. Take a long thread through a bead and through horizontal bead A of bottom row. Thread another bead and take thread through horizontal bead B of 24-bead row. Add another bead and continue threading the 2 rows together. Leave threads at both ends. Knot these to the 24-bead row threads. Paint beads red, blue, purple and gold.

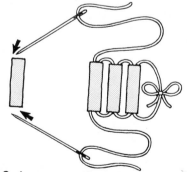

2nd row: use both needles with long pieces of thread. Thread 1 needle into top of a bead and the other into the bottom. Thread needles up and down through 52 beads. Leave threads tied in bows at both ends of row.

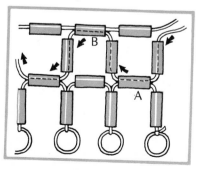

Untie all the bows. Thread ends through folds in bird's head clasps and glue in place. Fold clasps over and glue together. Tie 2 pieces of cord through loops on clasps.

AN EGYPTIAN MUMMY'S CASKET

The Ancient Egyptians believed that after death they would go to another world where they would enjoy the pleasantest moments of their time on Earth. They thought that the spirit would need the earthly body in the afterlife, so they mummified the bodies of the dead.

To preserve the body in this way the internal organs were removed and the body dried with salts and spices. Then it was wrapped round with linen. The final layer of linen was treated with preservative.

The mummified body of a wealthy person was placed in a wooden casket, which might have been designed to look like a human body. The casket was elaborately decorated and inscribed with hieroglyphics—sign writing—telling of the good things in this world in the hope that the dead person would enjoy them in the next.

How to make the casket

Materials: cardboard, gummed paper strip, pencil, scissors, ruler, glue, paint, paintbrush

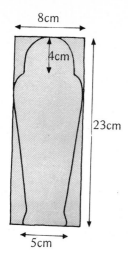

Draw casket outline A on cardboard rectangle 23 x 8cm. Cut out shape. Draw 2 more casket shapes by placing shape A on cardboard and drawing round it. Cut out shapes following outside edge of line. These 2 lid shapes, B and C, should be slightly larger than A.

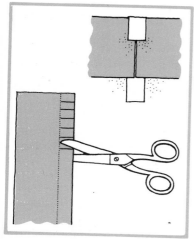

Cut strips of card 40cm wide for casket sides. If necessary, join strips with gummed paper strip. Score a line down strips 1cm from edge. Cut slits into strips.

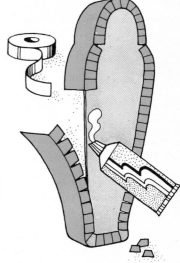

Bend strip around casket base A. Fold tabs over and glue to base. Cut away tabs at corners of casket foot. Joint strip with gummed paper strip.

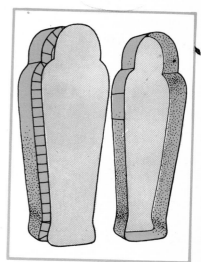

Make casket lid in same way, using shape B. Glue shape C on top of casket lid, covering tabs. Paint and decorate the casket.

AN EGYPTIAN SHADUF

Egypt is a desert country and farmers have always depended on the River Nile for water to irrigate their crops. They take the water either direct from the river or from the irrigation canals that lead between the fields. As the fields are often above the level of the water, the Egyptians have had to use various methods to raise the water. One method, invented by the Ancient Egyptians and still used occasionally today, is the shaduf.

The shaduf is a simple device. It consists of a long pole balanced on a cross beam. At one end of the pole are a rope and bucket, at the other end a heavy counterweight, usually a mud ball. The people pull the bucket to the canal or river and fill it with water. The counterweight raises the bucket and the water can easily be emptied into one of the narrow ditches that run among the crops.

How to make the Shaduf

Materials: thin wooden dowel, sweets tube, Plasticine, plastic carton, matchstick, string, craft knife, 10cm cardboard square, scissors, ruler, glue, paint, paintbrush

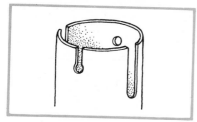

Cut a 3cm and 2cm slot in opposite sides of tube. At right angles to slots make 2 holes for matchstick just below tube rim. Cut slot from rim to 1 hole.

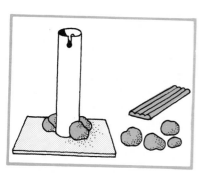

Glue tube onto cardboard square. Model some Plasticine stones. Press them around tube base.

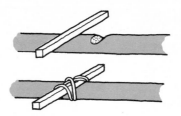

Cut dowel 45cm long. Cut a notch 14cm from 1 end. Glue matchstick in notch, bind to dowel with string.

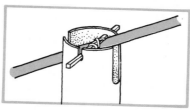

Slip matchstick through hole in tube and into slot. The short length of dowel should fit into the long slot in tube.

Cut a small plastic carton in half. Make 3 equidistant holes around top. Cut two 12cm lengths of string. Thread one piece through 2 holes and tie it onto carton.

Thread other piece of string through third hole. Tie it onto carton, round other piece of string and onto end of dowel. Paint tube and carton.

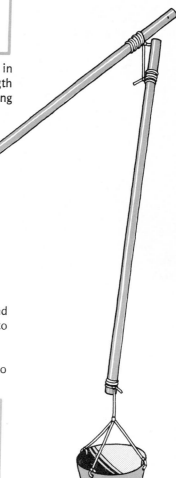

Press a Plasticine weight onto end of dowel. Tie a piece of string to other end.

Cut dowel 25cm long. Tie it onto end of long dowel.

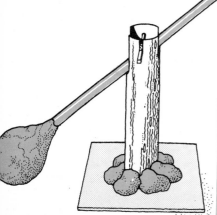

23

AN EARLY GREEK TEMPLE

Although the early Greek temples were small, architects had already introduced the idea of columns that later made great temples such as the Parthenon so magnificent. The porches on these small early temples were supported on two columns. The roof rested on other columns set against the walls. It was made of clay tiles and was highly patterned. The walls were made of oblong stone blocks decorated with religious murals or inscribed with religious laws. The temple windows were small triangles set high in the walls.

Each temple was dedicated to a different god. The main form of religious worship in ancient Greece was the sacrifice of an animal at the altar inside the temple.

How to make the temple

Materials: cardboard box, shoe box lid, covered corrugated cardboard, sweets tubes, pencil, ruler, craft knife, glue, paint, paintbrush

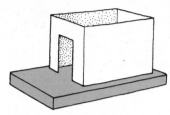

Find or make a cardboard box 18 x 13 x 12cm. Cut out a door and 4 triangular windows. Glue box onto shoe box lid.

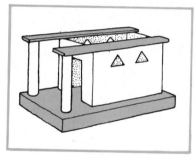

Cut 2 covered corrugated cardboard strips 27 x 6cm. Score each one down centre, fold in half and glue together. Glue strips onto box overlapping 8cm at front, 1cm at back and 5mm along sides. Glue 2 sweets tubes between base and strips.

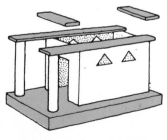

Cut 2 strips 8 x 6cm. Score down centre, fold and glue together. Glue strips onto box overlapping the ends by 5mm.

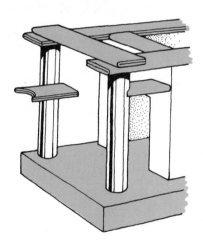

Cut a strip 14 x 6cm. Score down centre, fold and glue together. Glue onto strips above columns. Cut 2 strips 5 x 6cm. Score down centre, fold and glue together. Shape 1 end of strips to fit around columns. Glue strips in place 3cm from top of columns.

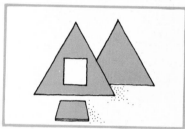

Cut 2 triangular cardboard gables 10cm high and 12cm wide at base. Cut 4cm square window in 1 gable.

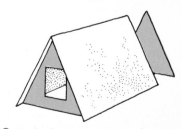

Cut cardboard rectangle 23.5 x 18cm. Score down centre and fold to form roof. Glue gables within ends of roof. Glue roof onto model. Paint and decorate the temple.

A GREEK CAVALRY SWORD

The early Greek cavalry swords were made of bronze, an alloy of copper and tin. The Greeks used bronze because copper is much easier to smelt than iron. Later, when their techniques improved, they made their weapons of iron.

Greek cavalry swords, with their single edged, slightly curved blades, were clearly meant for downward slashing strokes. The swordmaker hammered out the blade and narrowed the handle to a thin, but strong, point. He then tapped the crossguard on until it fitted securely. The hilt was made of wood or carved ivory. It was designed to be gripped for a downward stroke.

How to make the sword

Materials: cardboard, plastic foam tile, 8 drawing pins, tracing paper, pencil, ruler, glue, craft knife, paint, paintbrush

Draw rectangle 44 x 8cm on tracing paper. Divide into 2cm squares. Draw in sword shape.

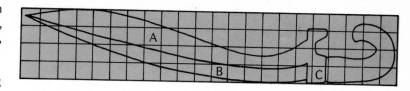

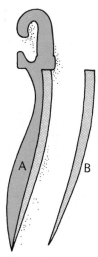

Trace outline of blade and handle (A) onto cardboard. Cut out shape. Trace 2 outlines of blade section (B) onto cardboard. Cut out shapes. Glue 1 shape on each side of sword blade.

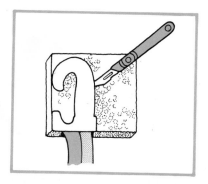

Glue sword handle onto plastic foam tile. Cut round edge with sharp craft knife. Glue another piece of plastic foam tile to other side of sword handle. Cut round the edge.

Trace 2 outlines of guard (C) onto cardboard. Cut out shapes and glue them onto sword.

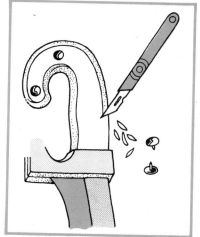

Carefully round off handle edges with a craft knife. Paint the sword. Press drawing pins into each side of handle.

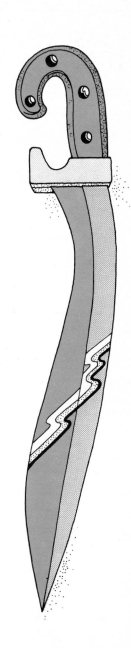

AN ANCIENT GREEK HELMET

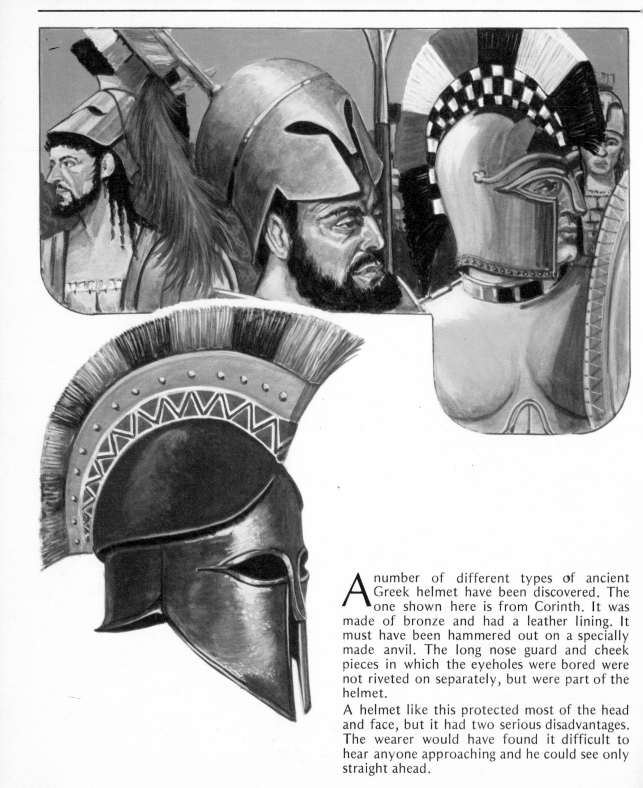

A number of different types of ancient Greek helmet have been discovered. The one shown here is from Corinth. It was made of bronze and had a leather lining. It must have been hammered out on a specially made anvil. The long nose guard and cheek pieces in which the eyeholes were bored were not riveted on separately, but were part of the helmet.

A helmet like this protected most of the head and face, but it had two serious disadvantages. The wearer would have found it difficult to hear anyone approaching and he could see only straight ahead.

How to make the helmet

Materials: cardboard, cardboard tube, newspaper, glue, wallpaper paste, pencil, scissors, paint, paintbrush

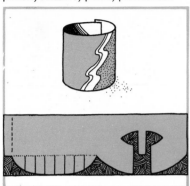

Cut a cardboard rectangle and bend it into a tube that will fit over your head. Open tube out flat and draw in helmet shape. Cut out shaded parts. Cut slits at each side along bottom edge.

Bend helmet shape into tube again. Glue edges together. Fold flaps along bottom edge outwards. Tear some newspaper strips. Use wallpaper paste to cover flaps with 3 layers of strips.

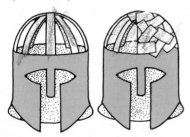

Cut 4 cardboard strips and glue them onto helmet to form dome. Paste several layers of newspaper strips over dome. Allow to dry thoroughly.

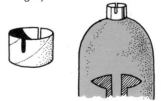

Cut a 3cm length of cardboard tube. Make 2 slits in top. Glue tube onto helmet with slits at front and back.

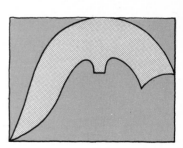

Cut crest from cardboard rectangle 29 x 41cm. Fit crest into slits in tube and glue in place. Paint and decorate the helmet.

29

AN IRON AGE HUT

The types of houses built during the Iron Age depended on the materials available locally. Some were made entirely of stone, others of wood and skins, and many of wood and stone.

The early houses were usually circular, and about 5 metres across. The builders dug a shallow pit and lined the floor with large flat stones. They raised one stone above the others to use later as a hearthstone. Then they built a stone wall about one metre high, buttressed by floor slabs at the front and an earthen bank at the back. The entrance was a stone lintel supported on two vertical slabs.

The roof timbers rested on the wall and leaned forward to a central post. Thin branches were woven between the timbers, and the whole was covered with turf or thatch to make it waterproof. A smokehole was left in the top.

How to make the hut

Materials: cardboard, Plasticine, drinking straws, curved needle, string, brown wrapping paper, ruler, compasses, scissors, glue

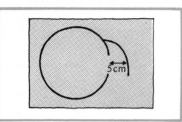

Cut cardboard base 20 x 28cm. Draw circle with 16cm diameter for hut outline on base. Leave 4cm space for doorway. Draw curved line 5cm from doorway for covered entrance.

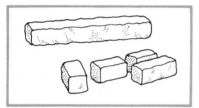

Model long Plasticine blocks 1cm square. Cut off irregular lengths for building stones.

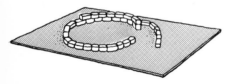

Following outline, press a layer of Plasticine stones on base. Add 2 more layers. Make 3 large stones 4cm x 1cm x 5mm for door arch.

Press a lump of Plasticine on base in middle of hut.

Fit a pencil 12cm long into the lump of Plasticine.

Cut 13 straws to 12cm, and 2 straws to 10cm for hut roof. Trim ends diagonally.

Press shorter straws into door lintel and glue them to pencil tip. Press other straws into Plasticine stones and glue to pencil.

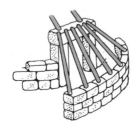

Cut 5 straws 6cm long. Trim ends diagonally. Press straws into entrance wall and lintel.

Use curved needle to loosely weave string through straws, starting at top. Weave entrance separately.

Cut pieces of brown paper about 4 x 2cm. Cut fringes into paper. Glue fringes in overlapping layers onto entrance, and then main, roof.

Cut circular brown paper fringe 6cm in diameter. Cut into circle and cut small hole in centre. Fold into cone to fit on top of roof. Glue in place.

First published in Great Britain 1978 by Owlet Books, Mills & Boon
Limited, 17-19 Foley Street, London W1A 1DR.

Owlet Books
© Mills & Boon Ltd 1978

THE ANCIENT WORLD   ISBN 0 263 06335 6

Printed in Italy